Vaccines for Violence

Frances Henry

Illustrations by Walter Korzec

EAST BRANCH PRESS
Cummington, Massachusetts

PREVIOUS PUBLICATIONS BY THE AUTHOR

Toughing It Out at Harvard: The Making of A Woman MBA

Flame Jewel Friend: A Triptych on Loss & Love

East Branch Press
P.O. Box 152
Cummington, Massachusetts

www.eastbranchpress.com

ISBN 978-0-9776369-2-1

for
M.L.R. & J.A.M.
mentors
colleagues
friends

TABLE OF CONTENTS

Vaccines for Violence...3

Make Peace with Fear...13

Balance Accountability with Compassion...25

Faith and Reason...37

Patrons of Possibility...49

Chance favors the prepared mind.

Louis Pasteur

Vaccines for Violence

VACCINES FOR VIOLENCE

COULD anything have been more ordinary in the early 1960s than a teen-aged daughter helping her mother prepare dinner for a family of six? In my case, Mom phoned every afternoon from her secretary's desk at a law office on Main Street in Sag Harbor, New York and told me to make the potatoes scalloped or mashed, and whether or not to open a package of frozen peas. Sometimes she let me make a bowl of Jell-O. When she arrived home an hour later, our family gathered promptly for the evening meal, and I felt pleasure at helping her feed the brood.

But little else seemed routine in that decade, and especially one afternoon when I jolted our evening ritual with a question.

"Ma, if the atom bomb lands on New York City, what are you going to do with us?"

That day I had overheard my history teacher whispering in the hallway to my science teacher—*Russians, Cuba, warships*. I knew they were frightened and what caused it.

Without pause as she stirred flour into the gravy, Mom turned slowly toward me, "Why Fran, I would take all of you right down to Noyack Bay and drown you."

And that was how as a child I learned that one act of violence would lead to the next. Now I wonder what our world had come to: a mother's best hope of protecting her children was to kill them.

My education in violence started years before this conversation and went on long after. My life felt steeped in the physical violence of one parent, the sexual violence of the other. By middle school, I had spent years responding to the alarms from air raid systems, learning how to duck under my desk, and to shield my face from blown glass if disaster struck. Through the media I inhaled a steady stream of toxic images such as rioting in cities across America, police shooting students on a college campus, and assassinations of leaders.

Then by the 1970s, as the Vietnam War ended and I entered my twenties, I became prey to the widespread epidemic of robbery and personal attacks which erupted in many cities. One time, when driving in Washington, D.C. with a friend, my car lost power and we pulled off the road. A man who had been biking stopped, chatted, and helped to fix the car. After he left, we were shocked to find that he had stolen my wallet. Another time young men mugged me at knife-point.

Soon after one of these thefts, I attended a concert at which Joan Baez sang—as only she could—about opening the prison doors and letting everyone go. I didn't agree. I wanted someone to hold those men accountable. Yet, like Baez, I knew that bars locked in the problem of crime and violence, but did not hold the key to its solution.

More than another quarter century is now gone. I have been living with what violence has wrought for nearly sixty years. If I were the only victim, I could bear the cost. Instead, more than one and a half million die each year from violence and millions more are devastated by it. People across the globe suffer as if from a plague and my thinking comes to this: no one in their right mind wakes up hoping they will have a violence-soaked day. No one brings an infant into this world praying to fill their child's days with abuse. And yet, so many of us accept violence as part of the human condition. Absent vision, who possesses the strength to see the problem through to its solutions? Who among us musters the will to change?

I find courage in my search to prevent violence when I seek other people who have harnessed their imaginations in the service of change. I turn, for example, to Dr. Louis Pasteur.

Dr. Pasteur in 1821 advanced germ theory and proposed inoculation to build up antibodies and immunity to infectious disease. Scientists took another one hundred years to develop the first vaccine, but by the turn of our millennium, medicine offered vaccines for all eleven of the major childhood killers like smallpox and polio, measles and mumps. Today, ninety-nine percent of the sicknesses that would have been caused by those infections are prevented. In industrialized countries, doctors immunize widely and most children live until adulthood. Yet, just two hundred years ago, many parents lost their infants and young children to infectious disease. In poor countries, they still do.

So think about it. Think about all of those parents for so many generations grieving the loss of their babies and children, powerless before the symptoms, the course of the illness, and its outcome. They must have believed that disease was inevitable, not preventable.

And so it is with violence. Violence travels like the microbes that cause disease—in the news, in the movies, in the home, and in each other. And it strikes like a disease—spread from one person, group, or country to another in an endless cycle of hurt.

We stumble about in an era like the one before doctors could peer into a microscope to see the causes of disease. Instead of looking at the origins of violence, some people use shame to change another's behavior. Others of us attribute violent acts to moral flaws and say religion will bring God's grace and heal people of their sins. Others, still, search for political and human rights solutions, arguing correctly that no one should be a victim of another's abuse. We fill our jails with those who do not respect that right. But while the rule of law provides a foundation, alone it will not end violence. When we punish after the fact, we do not probe or treat causes.

Moral and political approaches are necessary, but not sufficient to prevent violence. As practitioners of medicine did long ago before the advent of germ theory, we help as best we can when we deal with symptoms. But could we don a doctor's coat and become Louis Pasteur?

Long before the medical system existed, Pasteur used foresight to assume childhood health, not disease, was the human condition. So, too, we must conceive that vitality, not violence, constitutes our birthright. We must look deeply into biological, behavioral and social causes of violence. Using a cool head of reason and a warm heart of caring, we must discover and promote vaccines for violence.

What would a vaccine for violence look like?

Scientists have found that without attachment, babies will not thrive and children will become aggressive. Studies by social psychologists have shown that adolescents randomly placed in groups can be taught to compete in a way that escalates to violence or they can be taught skills of empathy and cooperation. Other studies have proven that adults become vulnerable to abuse by others when they are isolated and lack social networks.

From my own experience with abuse, I know that people who suffer violence can live with a pain so intense and so hidden, it destroys their ability to allow the human touch. I have lived with such a handicap, and I wonder if societies suffer in a similar manner. Can it be that we are unable to deal with the rage, grief and fear that surface in the face of the violence we have, individually and collectively, already experienced? Is it possible that we mistake violence as part of the human condition when instead our lives are scarred by the millions among us who lack capacity for secure attachment?

I vaccinate myself from becoming violent when I connect to another person. Like a series of building blocks, I connect first to myself through awareness of my needs, then connect to others through observing what they need. I connect to people in my community, and then to my nation and to the healthy values my society holds.

I don't assume that connecting alone will prevent violence. Society must attend both to an individual's acts and to his or her environment. Drawing upon the model of curing infectious disease, I keep in mind how scientists look not only for vaccines, but for all the causes of infections that spread through populations. Governments take responsibility for eliminating exposure to sewage, to water and airborne viruses, to the exchanges of body fluids, and to exposure to sick animals and birds. In this way, human ingenuity confronts the devastation of infectious disease, dismantles it, and lays out a plan for eradication. If our society held a similar spirit of inquiry about violence, people would open themselves to multiple paths to inoculate against it. They would look for a more wholesome society to surround them. Perhaps they would demand media and messages that are health-giving. If violence entertains them, they would ask why.

More people would learn skills of conflict resolution, so that differences of opinion did not erupt into violent behavior. For example, more of us would become expert at recognizing bullying behavior in children, adults or groups and develop skillful ways of diffusing it, or if need be, containing it.

More of us would learn about and support programs that have proven to lessen violence. For example, when nurses trained in parenting skills visit young, first-time mothers during pregnancy and for two years after birth, their children grow up to resist violent behaviors more often than children not given such social support. In impoverished townships of South Africa, women given social and economic incentives have remained fifty percent more free of domestic violence and HIV infection than women not given such help.

People would appreciate that jobs and economic well-being become vaccines for violence because poverty, especially along side wealth, correlates with violence.

People would understand the role that law enforcement and criminal justice systems need to play to provide the right dosage of accountability that violent acts require. We would help these systems build connection and relationship instead of severing it. And citizens would support governments that provide prevention programs for those who are vulnerable to perpetrating or being victimized by violence.

Thinking back to my childhood and my fear of a bomb falling on New York City makes me wonder about the nature of my parents' capacity to form attachment and also their ignorance about the violence they acted- out and contemplated. What had my mother experienced that frightened her enough to consider drowning her children? Perhaps she and my father discussed his last experiences in World War II. He spoke to me about it only once, on the fifty year anniversary of the dropping of the bomb on Japan.

He was one of the few to behold what the United States had wrought in 1945. As an enlisted sailor on the Navy ship that entered the harbor of Nagasaki just after that deadly act, my father's job allowed a peek through the slightly open door of the engine room, just enough to take in the sweeping

180 degree expanse—twisted remnants of buildings, wisps of smoke, and bodies floating next to debris. He had seen what humans could do to one another: "I have seen into hell. Something that cuts that deep, Fran, you never forget." I think of my parents and their abusive actions and I wonder, what else were they to do? Would I have acted any differently if I had lived their lives? I think not.

Perhaps facing violence with a new attitude feels impossible, as if what one person can do could never be enough. Yet if we bring ourselves to a problem with good intention and give of ourselves, it is plenty. I find inspiration, again, in the talent and imagination of one who came before me: Dante Alighieri, who wrote *The Divine Comedy* seven hundred years ago. Dante offered himself as a pilgrim for truth into human behavior and its consequences.

Stunning by virtue of its language and metaphor, his allegory takes the reader through horrifying realms of hell and purgatory finally to achieve paradise. At the beginning of his journey, when stepping through the doorway of hell, Dante glanced up to read a chilling inscription chiseled into the stone. It ended with the warning: "Abandon all hope ye who enter here." Traveling down spiral after spiral, the reader looks over the author's shoulder to see souls trapped by their greed, hatred, and jealousy.

But Dante could not attempt the roiling landscape alone. He beckoned his venerable mentor Virgil as a guide to the descent and Beatrice, a woman he loved, to serve as muse for the journey. In that gesture, he gifted humanity with the recognition that we need more than knowledge to brave the unknown. We need the human touch. We need connection.

Dante charted the terrain for how the rest of us can confront the awful and keep going until we find the good. We can find a guide who will breathe life into our vision, more even than a hope, of searching for and finding the vaccines for violence. Together we will witness the power that flows when we face the worst humans create and change it.

When I use my intelligence and my heart in the service of preventing violence, I feel a surge of power course through me. The task which once engulfed me instead bugles a wake-up call. What I do, what each of us does to connect to others in our daily life feeds not only us, but the life in our families, in our community, in the body of our nation and who we become as a people.

MAKE PEACE WITH FEAR

MY LEGS trembled as I stood to talk to Bella Abzug, Congresswoman of the United States and mentor to the governmental women's movement in the late 1970s. She had created an organization through an act of Congress to advance women's status. Bella chaired the group of commissioners, legends among them like Gloria Steinem and Coretta Scott King. I had been hired for a junior position, but I had assumed senior management tasks to run parts of the meeting. We had all created a whirlwind of work which called 15,000 people to Houston, Texas for a national women's conference in 1977.

Donning the hat that became her trademark, Bella led us with commitment and inspiration. But she also could be punishing in her outbursts, blaming others when she did not get her way. I once took the blow when she screamed at me for not being able to control a group of people who threatened her plans. Like most of us, I tried to do my job and stay out of her way.

After the staff had completed its public work in Houston, Bella gathered a few dozen of us in our offices in Washington, D.C. and now they surrounded me. She spoke with appreciation for our heroic effort. But something jarred in me as she spoke. It may have been that, knowing her bluster, I did not trust her praise. Or I may have been remembering Bella's actions at the end of the conference a few weeks before: with many thousands watching, she had called a few of us, including me, up to the podium. She thanked those few grandly and ignored all of the rest who had worked just as hard. Our efforts had been about creating a common bond of equality, and I had not liked being singled out for praise if others were neglected. In both cases, her appreciation felt hollow to me.

I recalled, too, in those moments, a recent nightmare I had about Bella in which I had been badly hurt. I knew she stood for something in my own psyche that was wounded and needed attention. Part of me wanted to avoid the situation but another part knew I had to face her.

I stood to speak. Fear vibrated inside me and rose in my throat. Would she unleash her wrath again? Without anger or malice, I explained my position—that she was not an easy person to work for and that we were not all treated equally well. I spoke what weighed on my heart.

Bella shifted from one foot to another and then, raising her hand and closing it on the wide felt brim, lifted her hat. I had never seen Bella's head! Hatless, she struck a much less frightening presence and each one in the room sensed it. She thanked me for speaking, apologized to everyone, and said she had meant no harm. The moment passed, she settled the hat on its rightful perch, and the meeting focused on other business. But something in me had shifted.

Did I grow an inch? No, but my stature swelled to encompass the power of speaking without shaming or blaming, and the opening it gives to another person for a measured response. I learned something else, too. Confronting the Bella of my nightmare helped me to make conscious and then to dissipate her looming, dangerous presence in my psyche. I thought about my fear of the Bella I knew and the Bella of my dream and how they had merged. It made me wonder what else I might be afraid of and how I might inflate that fear. Perhaps when I am hurt, as I had been by Bella's rages, my level of anxiety escalates and my reason clouds.

Once I became aware of how I felt, I could describe how Bella's behavior troubled me. By acting on what I knew, my fears, real and projected, had less material to feed upon. Once I spoke, both Bella and I could move on. But if I hadn't, what bitterness might have festered in me? What might have ripened so that I, too, treated someone poorly in a similar situation? Further, what drove Bella to her behavior? Did unknown fears lurk in her? Bella's verbal abuse measures tame on a continuum of violent acts that includes beating, rape or murder, but what if the most scorching forms of violence could be traced back to mild fears which spiral beyond a person's or a society's capacity to contain them?

Looking back to that period three decades ago, I can see I was learning that if I engaged fear, it would not control me. But recently I unearthed a time even further back, ten years before Bella, when I had not yet learned that lesson. My discovery happened when the Sophia Smith Collection at Smith College asked for "my papers" to add to their collection of original material by women. Before I turned over the half a dozen boxes of letters I had carried to each of the twenty places I had lived as a young adult, I wanted to read them again, to cull those too intimate for anyone but me. Combing through the cartons, I came to a sheaf between me and a man I had met in college and who later became my husband. We had fallen in love in 1968, had trekked to Woodstock together, and had attended marches on civil rights. We had lived in the East Village in New York City where, on New Year's Eve in 1969 at the Fillmore East, we heard Jimi Hendrix blast my generation into the 1970s.

In the first year of our relationship when we lived on separate campuses, we had sent poems or letters to each other. As I looked again at his striking penmanship, I was wrenched back into those years. I had found him beautiful. We dated, married and then a few years later, divorced. For thirty years, I had believed what I told him as I left: "I wish you could express yourself and tell me that you love me." It had seemed so clear.

Now I had his letters in my hands again, tied together with silver ribbons and long ago tucked into a folder. Reading through them, I was not prepared to discover how he used my nickname over and over, as if it were a mantra. There must have been four dozen poems and letters, a few sketches, and another dozen scraps and notes that he had left for me on the kitchen table or in my book bag, notes that reminded me to button my coat or to remember how he felt. He wrote about how my love had opened him to a world he had never explored. Then I read the last letter he sent, the one after I had left. In it he said he would not forget me, that he wanted me to be happy, and that he released me from our marriage. Who was that man?

I slowly bundled the letters, feeling queasy. I thought I had known the truth and formed my beliefs around it. Now I was not so sure. I dug deeper, into the bottom of the box, biting my lip and then sitting up straight. There was another envelope. I had forgotten about these letters, too; mine sent to him. He had saved my letters! Once we married, we combined our possessions, but perhaps we had not looked in this box when we separated, or perhaps he had not wanted them.

Each letter pushed me further back into a part of myself I do not like to explore. In one, I loved him and said so. In the next letter, I drew back and told him he should leave me, that I was not sure what I felt. The back and forth of it set my head spinning, not because I did not recognize the woman who wrote those words, but because I realized that through all my vacillations, he wrote letter after letter describing the warmth in his heart. With a piercing ache, I now realized that long ago I had been too scared to receive his love. Instead of understanding my fear, I had faulted him.

Over the decades since I ended that relationship, I have come to better know myself. I understand now that I live in fear of happiness, yearning for it, but being able to tolerate the longing more than the possibility of loving and losing. Love requires admitting how much someone's connection means and I was not willing to explore that territory in my young self, with my young husband. I felt fright at being cared for, fright at caring for another. What a contrast to how I handled the relationship to Bella when I admitted fear to myself, spoke it and let it go, building rather than destroying connection.

Because of what I have learned from a lifetime of turning toward fear, I am now far more able to contain it rather than being pushed and pulled by it. This is true even when the things I fear seem more harrowing than my experience with Bella. I remember a morning about fifteen years ago when I entered my office to flick the light switch, open the windows, and pause to boot the computer. In less than a minute, I had begun the ritual of starting a day at work; yet it was a day different from any previous. This steamy morning in July marked the first of my full time effort to launch and run an organization I founded to help prevent the sexual abuse of children.

I turned to the blinking answering machine on my desk and pressed the button to listen to messages: just one. Perhaps my husband or a friend had left a note of encouragement.

Instead I heard raspy, heavy breathing. A gasp. Glued to the floor, I listened. Then a thin, pleading voice: "I.....I can't stop myself." Click.

I knew instantly that the caller had read an article in the local paper a few days before. I had been interviewed about my ideas for reaching out to people who abuse and to families where children might be victimized. But I also thought he responded to the name of the organization, "Stop It Now!," and he was admitting what so few people with addictive behaviors can admit: they cannot easily stop what they start.

A surge of panic engulfed me. What *had* I begun? What would I bring upon myself? Upon others? At that moment all my ideas about treatment and about the ways to get people help before they harm someone felt useless. I felt pinned by his desperation.

I could not focus on my work. This man had unwittingly drawn out of me the fears I harbored inside about being vulnerable to people who had more power than I had— people who would harm me if they could. I wanted to protect myself—to quit that instant. But then I thought about why

I had taken the risks I had—to foster strength in families so they could prevent their children from being compromised. I hoped that if I set my fears aside for the moment, I would figure out what to do. So I spent the day as I had planned; I arranged meetings in Washington, D.C., read research studies on prevention methods, and acted as if the call had not happened.

By the end of the day, I could revisit my fear, allowing other thoughts to emerge. Certainly the call was the reason I was afraid. But what even deeper fears did that call uncork? It would take time to understand those, but first, at the surface, I felt unglued at the possibility of being harmed in the course of my work. With that awareness, I could calm myself, because I knew that if I felt unsafe, I could change it. I could call the police in the small town where my office was located. When I dialed their number and reached the officer on duty, I told him that I ran a program which put me in touch with difficult, perhaps even dangerous people. I asked if their office would help me if I ever called in an emergency. The fellow told me to call 9-1-1, but he also let me know that, yes, his office would respond.

I thought more about that message later in the week. I realized that the caller had galvanized my fears because I worked alone. I had taken every bit of resources and savings to get my organization started. I had no money for staff and depended on volunteers and a part-time consultant. In my daily work, the people I called or wrote lived far away.

Had I unwittingly created isolation, forming a place for fear to feed? Perhaps I hearkened back to being a child when I had been so alone with all of the impossible demands that had been placed on me. I did not have to separate myself now. I wrote twenty of my closest allies and asked each one to call me during a different week over the next six months. I asked the friend to call once or twice during that week, just to see how I was or to leave a message. All of them agreed and nineteen remembered to call. I soaked up their caring and when the twenty weeks had passed, I found I no longer needed the attention. By offering them a chance to reach toward me, I had addressed the fear that phone message had evoked.

Perhaps a year or more later, once my ideas had emerged into a program and an organization, I came to understand another meaning for my reaction to that phone call. By then I had received a range of responses to the program, many of them skeptical, some even hostile. In journal entries day after day, I scribbled a raw terror: Would society be able to hear about harmful sexual behavior without denying the problem or calling for castration? Would people change enough to protect children? Was I fostering a helpful solution or bringing on more harm?

I came to understand that on very difficult social issues, society itself holds a kind of collective fear, perhaps an accumulation of all the individual fears that most of us suffer. When someone comes forward with fresh thoughts, as I had in the arena of child sexual abuse, others can lash out. In the process, the new idea can wither. But when an individual becomes aware of her fear, her anger, or her doubt and, mastering it, acts from a wholesome place, ripples fan out into the larger community. None of us can know when one ripple will join with others to form a wave of human possibility.

To master fear, I have learned to turn toward it. I face it best when I am strong and can take the time to think without acting. I take my mind as far as I can to the source of the fear, answering the questions: of what am I afraid? and what might be behind that? With awareness comes kindness to myself, because I understand that the fear tries to shield me from harm. Then I strike a bargain by simultaneously giving my fear space to exist and circling it.

When I am not able to face fear, I need to surround it with my compassion. I tend the feeling like a mother might a child, admitting that I hurt, soothing myself. If the fear covers a deep wound, it might need even more care, perhaps being nourished by my tears.

At still other times, when I need to act and to be clear-headed about a decision, facing or calming fear is not the solution. I must call on courage to admit the fear but park it. I need to act as if the fear is baseless. I can't seek solace; I must move forward as if my fears do not exist. Putting my capacity for reason aside, I withdraw my intellect and my attention. But I do not let anxiety fill its place. I feel almost as if I lift myself up and over the fears, leaving them at my feet.

When people are afraid, they can act violently, which in its turn breeds more fear, breeding more violence, on and on for millennia. I have seen this myself: violence maims and kills. When I have responded in fear, I have become numb or aggressive. I have not hurt anyone physically, but I have severed relationships abruptly, unkindly. When I allow the emotional space inside me to flood with fear, the world outside me becomes a place to be afraid of.

Mahatma Gandhi realized that distrust is a sign of weakness, especially when one's goal is to win over, rather than to destroy. Gandhi knew that trust builds inner strength of character and so he cultivated it. He knew that when he was resolute inside himself, he was not affected by what happened around him. He was not mislead by fear of suffering. We do not have to be a Gandhi to follow his example. If we could bolster our capacity to be resolute and to trust, violence throughout the world would change.

In my life, I face fear with connection. When I am afraid of the connection itself, I cannot succeed, as was the case in my youthful marriage. Fear dominated and won. Each of us could value our feelings of connection. If we are subject to violence that breaks the connection, if we are betrayed or if someone we love is attacked, or even if our community or our country is at risk for war, at each of these levels, we can become awake to what will restore the bond. Our actions might take the form of standing up for what we know is true, as in my shake-kneed conversation with Bella. We might need to keep our heart open even when we are rejected, as did my husband those many years ago. Perhaps we need to put our fears on hold while we accomplish the task at hand, as I did on a hot day in July.

I do not pretend as if I have found the answer. I negotiate the raw edge of my fears every day. If I am quiet when I wake in the morning, I can hear a subtle, disturbing hum. It vibrates like a note on a stringed instrument, infinitely resonating in the chamber of my heart. The underlying sound of my existence contains a measure of fear, perhaps arising from my animal biology or my early life experiences. Conceivably, all humans live with such a hum, the same and different from mine.

Waking to that drone of fear, I can make peace with it. It does not have to dictate the course of my life. I sense it, rouse myself from sleep, pull on layers of wool and down, and step into the frosty morning. Inhaling deeply, I take in the sparkle of a new day. I do not leave fear behind, just a fear-based life.

BALANCE ACCOUNTABILITY
WITH COMPASSION

• ● ● ● ● ● ● ● ● ● ● ● ● ● ●

FOR YEARS, I wrestled with whether or not to send a card to my Pop on Father's Day. I was not alone, I'm sure, among other adults who grew up in homes where we were hit or sexually assaulted, belittled, neglected, or lived in the chaos of addictions or violence. What were we to do—ignore the past? Ignore the holiday? Or buy a card: "Mom, Dad...You're The Greatest."

It took me decades to find a balance. One year before I had, I sent a Father's Day greeting with a note about my ambivalence. He called me. "Listen, you don't have to send me anything for Father's Day, but if you do, don't tell me how hard it was and how much you struggled to do it. You set me up and it hurts."

I felt guarded. He had hurt me for years. What right did he have now to say I shouldn't hurt him?

No matter our backgrounds, most of us are raised to pay homage to elders. I learned from what my parents said and also from lessons in the Bible: honor thy mother and father. Yet for me and for so many other children, people breached that commandment when it had to do with their prerogative and my rights. My mother hit me too often and too hard when I was a toddler. My father sexually assaulted me when I was a teenager. A decade ago, I suffered the anguish of a husband who killed himself.

Now that my work entails preventing violence, it demands that I learn about the seemingly endless ways that people can be violent to one another and to themselves. I have struggled with how to accept and heal from the damage of personal violence, how to redeem the past, and how to change the future.

When I was young, the violence struck like a billiard ball, spinning me round and sending me flying. Its whirling thwarted whoever I might have become and headed me in wholly other directions. Such course-changes took place at school. Mostly, I excelled. Yet when a teacher paid attention to me or my work, I cringed away from what felt like a glare, and moved to the edge of his classroom. In college, for example, I gobbled up history courses with a passion that had begun in junior high, but when my freshman history professor announced to the class that one student, me, had earned his rare A+ for the course, I switched my major.

I grew up altered in other ways, too. Violence wove shards of fear into my relationships with others. I parsed a rat's nest of feelings to understand a hard clenching of my heart. Then slowly over the decade of my twenties, things shifted inside me. I began to remember all that my parents had done well to raise their children. I admitted how much it meant to me that when I confronted my father as a teenager, he had not lied about his abuse, nor blamed me. I discovered that despite the harm, I still loved them. I felt compassion, opened my heart, and found the act of forgiveness waiting there. I could understand that they had hurt me out of something more powerful than their love—ignorance.

Then surprising to me, after I forgave them, anger erupted. The forgiveness became a ground upon which I steadied myself in order to feel the rage at how the abuse had affected me. Understanding that I loved them did not excuse their behavior. I wanted my parents to be accountable.

What did I mean by that? Most of us think immediately of judgment and punishment, but that seemed not what I was reaching for.

Somehow I had the faith that we could broach the past without knowing the outcome. I asked for another talk with my father and mother about what my father had done, and they agreed. I told them that I loved them, but I also wanted them to know what I had been through, and I wanted them to explain as much as possible about what had happened in our family. I needed to know that my father would never be alone with children. My parents listened. My father said again that what he did was his fault, not mine. He could not explain what drove him to abuse me.

The awkward painfulness of the conversations left each of us feeling raw, but talking brought me insight and eased my anger. It was about this time that I sent the honest, but troubling, message in my father's card. While at first I had defended myself against his response, as I thought about it, my father was right to call me on my hurtful behavior. Accountability goes both ways, and I realized after that phone conversation with my father that I still had a lot to learn.

In another visit with them soon after the phone call, I discovered how easily I might have misused the privilege of holding them accountable. I stepped through the back door as my parents came from the living room into the pocket-sized kitchen of my family home. On each of their faces I saw a look I had not seen before: fear! The truth I had brought home was now intimidating them and they showed it. I did not intend to make them afraid of me, but what was I to do?

At that moment my heart awakened with a quiver. I could feel a tenderness arise within me, unprecedented and alive with the frailty of their desire to have their daughter love them. In that visit and in others after, I took care to see that my actions did not give my parents reason to fear me again. Witnessing their vulnerability, I knew I needed to discover how to balance the accountability my mind required with the compassion quivering in my heart.

Holding people accountable is not like reconciling the statement from your bank with all the debits and credits coming to an equal sign. It can be messy. My parents had limits on how much they could see the abuse from my point of view. Sometimes that hurt because I still wanted them to transform into the empathic parents they had not been when I was small.

More significant, I needed to admit I was capable of punishing. But does punishment give me what I wish for in the first place: to prevent violence? Does it even work after the fact? Looking back on my experience, I longed for my parents to have gotten help with the stress of family life and the backgrounds they brought to it. Punishment held no purpose for me as it would come too late and lack meaning. Instead, holding other parents accountable to not hitting or sexually abusing their children—that was a goal I could work toward for other families.

By attending to what I learned in my family, I came to believe that accountability, fine tuned with compassion, is what transforms circumstances. If I hold someone accountable without feeling compassion for his or her circumstance, I risk seeking revenge or punishment for its own sake. But similarly, if I offer compassion without holding the person accountable, I have wrestled with only half the solution. Compassion generates an open heart, but that alone will not change the circumstances that gave rise to the harm.

Does choosing either accountability or compassion by itself create change? Not often enough. Instead, if we hold them simultaneously and contain the tension between these two principles, real change will ensue.

When people admit the truth of violent experiences, anger surfaces, as it did with me toward my parents. Fear or despair can emerge, too. These emotions, a form of shadow to the truth, can plunge any of us or an entire society into retaliatory behavior. I have seen too many situations where it feels easier to harm someone than deal with the pain of getting closer by grappling with the complexity of their life story.

Those of us who feel able must help our families and our societies contain the shadow, so that those emotions do not overwhelm us and drive our behavior. We contain the emotions by making them conscious, accepting them, and then bringing them to balance with our power to care and feel empathy. It takes practice. It takes a willingness to talk, to communicate.

Others have charted a path for us, providing ideas about how to balance accountability with compassion. I admire the principles that Alcoholics Anonymous uses in which people learn to not condemn the person with alcoholism, but instead to deal with the behavior of drinking. I have been a trainer in the Quaker program, Alternatives to Violence in which we teach people in prison to change life-long habits of acting violently by learning how instead to use simple, declarative statements about what we wanted from others. To be a trainer, one must master the practice in her own life.

I study the work of Marshall Rosenberg, who helps people see how conflict is a result of human needs that are not met.

In the political sphere, the principles of compassion and accountability averted the impending bloodbath when in South Africa, Nelson Mandela fostered Truth and Reconciliation Commissions to air the terror of apartheid, and in an atmosphere of respect, held people accountable. In the United States, we could experiment further with models of restorative justice in which the person harmed, the person harming, and the community attend to the wrong committed. Offenders usually meet with members of the community, sometimes with victims, and many times a form of restitution occurs through agreements, community service, and financial payments. We could research, evaluate and determine if this model leads to lower rates of people returning to prison.

Stop It Now!, an organization I founded to prevent the sexual abuse of children, created meetings in community centers that invited the public to hear from a panel of people who had experienced an abusive situation. The panel included a survivor, a family member, a therapist who treats sex offenders, and a person in recovery from offending. We opened the discussion for questions. At the end of every meeting, the audience spoke of how they had been changed by the power of confronting such terrifying behavior with factual information, respect, and firm commitments.

Balancing accountability with compassion does not mean others will change their behavior in every case. If a person tries to change, but commits a wrongdoing again, can I still have compassion and seek to understand them? I can because they tried. Suppose they did not try? I can still seek to be compassionate because if they are not able to try they must be terribly damaged inside or be surrounded by impossible conditions. I hold compassion because they exist in a hell realm, suffering in a way which cannot be measured. If someone commits crimes and cannot hold him or herself accountable to change, society must use its powers of protection and force by stepping in and acting for the wrongdoer.

Because I have spent many hours inside prison walls getting to know the people incarcerated there, I have developed compassion for them. I have learned that people are imprisoned because of their ignorance and selfishness and because of their life circumstances. Yet, I know that with the same circumstances or a different constitution I, too, might be one of these people. Prisoners have told me that people like me who care about them become like anchors when we hold out hope for a different future.

There are times when I cannot feel compassion for someone who harms. I want to protect myself from a person who might accept the compassion I have offered, and then commit another wrongdoing, perhaps even against me. Each one of us can control only our own behavior. We can encourage or cajole others, but no more. Sometimes we must have the courage to separate ourselves from someone's behavior, even from their presence. We might feel pangs of despair at our lack of power, but if we separate with compassion, we do not have to close our heart from the other.

At times I can feel defensive about balancing accountability with compassion, as if holding compassion means I let others off the hook. When I led Stop It Now!, I often answered reporters' questions about the organization's purpose and programs. In many interviews, the journalist asked, "Would your program reach so and so?," referring to the person who committed a recent heinous crime, perhaps a child abduction or worse. I always answered that preventing tomorrow's next murderous crime did not reside in reaching today's very ill people with a healing message. People who rampage and kill are thick with their chronic behavior. Such missives sail over their heads. The severely troubled person has cut him or herself off from relationships that could have healed. Now he or she needs containment. The roots of their front page story were planted long before, in their childhood or perhaps in an organic illness. To prevent the worst, we must invest in children today. We must reach children so that they learn to relate to others in life-affirming ways. Then the seeds of violence will not grow.

As I created ideas to prevent abuse from occurring in the next generations, I found that I could balance accountability and compassion in my own family. A few years ago my father entered his mid-eighties. I asked if he would meet with me and my siblings. The meeting would take place forty years after he had abused me and decades after my earliest attempts to wrestle with the abuse's effects on me. I hoped that my father would answer my siblings' questions and talk about his behavior to all of us. I hoped he could help us to establish a more honest family life for the rest of his life and ours.

All eight of us gathered in the living room after a Thanksgiving meal. As we took our places on the sofa, the floor, or, in my father's case, in the recliner, I am certain each of us wished we could be anywhere else but there. Yet perhaps we each harbored a private thought that this very meeting defined us as a family as much as any outing we had ever taken, any gifts we had ever given, or weddings we had attended. What had been shared in carefully worded private conversations finally would be spoken out loud, together.

Each of us wrestled with holding my father accountable. Any one of us could have dealt my father a withering blow. None did, though we had no agreement before about what to say or how to say it. Each of us found a way to listen to what he told us and to speak our own anger, fears, and finally, peace. At the end of the evening, spent though we were, we felt a gentle kindness for what we had been through. Toward the end of the conversation, my father asked if that meeting could be the last one of its type and I said, "Yes, Pop, we have all had the say we needed. Now we can move on." We have not needed to talk about it since.

With this meeting and the ones previous, I had transformed the commandment to honor my parent by acknowledging that the father I had as a child was not one who treated me with civility and love. By balancing accountability with compassion, I became a daughter who, despite my earlier experiences, could treat my father honorably. In doing so, my father was able to respond by treating me and my siblings the same way. The Father's Day holiday he had robbed me of as a child was restored.

Again I felt that sense of quivering, so subtle that I could miss it if I were not paying attention. Familiar: that same vibration that I recognized as fear at the beginning of our family meeting, returned at the end as love. I discovered that deep in our cells the body vibrates with the tension of an open heart like it quivers with fear when it wants to shut. The body will support us when we make the choice to step out of fear, and instead bring wrongs to right with an open heart.

FAITH AND REASON

FAITH infuses my life, yet I shrink from talking about it. Some suggest that spiritual matters do not translate into words. Fair enough, but not far enough. I fear the words. I do not want my truth to impinge on anyone else's. I recoil, too, from hasty judgments by people who dismiss matters of spirit. And, I shudder with the raw intimacy of faith revealing itself.

Long ago and for my earliest years, I felt that faith possessed sole truth. Then I discovered reason and left spiritual matters behind. Now I prefer a world where faith transcends a rote acceptance of religious belief and reason means more than the dry search for knowledge. Inside me now, faith and reason swirl in unison, but it has taken nearly a half-century for them to twine rather than to choke each other.

Three generations of my family filled the trades as secretaries, electricians, carpenters, and miners. For them and for three generations further back, as far as back I can trace my family's roots, no one had taken their schooling as far as college. But I thrived in school and from my earliest memories in kindergarten, I wanted as much of it as I could consume.

By my ninth year in school, I had taken standardized tests. The guidance counselor sent the scores to my parents with a note suggesting that they should send me to college. We had not discussed furthering my education and we did not know how to make it happen. But after that note, my mother took me aside for a heart-to-heart. "Fran, we will encourage you, but we have no extra money. You have to pay your own way. Maybe by studying, you can earn a scholarship."

We followed the directions the guidance counselor laid out for my future as a teacher and for my application to a state university. I rallied by earning a scholarship, by working from age fourteen, by saving money, and by arranging for a job and a loan at the college. By the fall of 1966 I felt ready for my first semester.

Even so, I could not have prepared for the minister's sermon the Sunday before I left home. The pastor called me to the altar, gave me the *New Testament in Modern English for Schools* and told me he had a special sermon for me and my family that day.

"Parents, beware of colleges and universities. They brainwash our children." My face burned with humiliation when I turned to the verse in II Timothy he had dedicated to me, "Steer clear of those unchristian babblings, which in practice lead further and further away from Christian teaching."

By the time of that sermon, the Christian teaching that had saturated my world view had already begun to sour. When I turned 13 my parents moved our family worship to a local evangelical church. Before that uprooting, my siblings and I had attended a Presbyterian Sunday School, where I had earned a ten-year pin for perfect attendance since age three. While part of me learned how to think by being challenged at public school, another part learned to believe as I had been taught in that first school: to find truth in the Bible.

Yet once I grew beyond early childhood, I had to face how much God had disappointed me. I had prayed for peace in my life at home, but mayhem reigned instead. I had taken heroes who spoke for truth: John Kennedy, Martin Luther King, Jr., Robert Kennedy. Their assassinations left me bereft and questioning the usefulness of relying on God's power.

John Kennedy held singular meaning for me. The country elected him on a November Tuesday in 1960 two days after my birthday. My mother clutched my hand as we walked across the street in our small town of Sag Harbor, New York. She entered Municipal Hall to vote for Richard Nixon. In what is my first memory of conscious, firm disagreement with my parent's world view, I knew that if I could, I would vote for Mr. Kennedy. I slipped my hand out of mom's and said, "Now I am twelve. You don't have to hold my hand anymore."

A few months later, I sat in rapt attention to the black and white scene on the twelve-inch screen in the television console in our living room. Thousands gathered around the Capitol steps in Washington, D.C. The wind blew President Kennedy's hair and everyone looked frozen in place, but his famous words radiated warmth into my home and heart. The new leader of the country sparked fledgling hopes for my own future. He called each of us to put aside our private concerns and to find how we could make our nation a better place.

My mother voted for Nixon, but the country had voted with me. I knew then that I need not be alone as I stepped out of childhood toward the world that Kennedy would lead. The juggle between faith and reason lodged itself within me as John Kennedy's election and his historic speech rooted the nation in its new place in the world. Six years later, as I listened to the minister's foreboding message, I might still have wanted to believe that God held dominion but sensed I had to leave that minister, that God, and the small church behind.

Then in 1968, when I was twenty and a junior in college, one book toppled the Bible for good and secured the pinnacle on my private intellectual mountain. *The Structure of Scientific Revolutions* by Thomas Kuhn explained how truth asserts itself in science. Through the scientific method, practitioners erect the case for a theory, one proof at a time. Paradigms shift when enough new facts emerge to disprove a current theory. I had not realized how hungry I had been for a fresh view on the world. Religion seemed to base itself in outmoded beliefs about things that may or may not have happened two thousand years ago. Science approached the world as it appeared and noted it. New observations meant new truths could emerge. I took Kuhn's book to mean that what I lived through in the 1960s—destruction of heroes, sexual violence, and war—could change. A tenet firmly established itself: new facts force old realities to fade away.

Decades later I founded Stop It Now!, an organization that used that tenet to forge a new path to prevent the sexual abuse of children. In the early 1990s, most people believed that only a few deranged people molest children, and society could dispatch those few by locking them in prison. The literature I read and the research Stop It Now! conducted with people who molested children told me a different truth. The systems of child protection and criminal justice dealt with abuse once it happened, but I questioned why society waited that long. The program I founded advanced the idea that the many, many millions of people who sexually offend against children could be prevented from doing so if we used the tools of the scientific method to understand their behavior and to extend hope and help to them and their families.

As I built the organization, I butted heads with established thinking about how to prevent harm to children and also met with some success. But real change seemed far away because only lock-them-up solutions attracted money and the media. People seemed to believe that sexual abuse was inevitable, not preventable. I needed to inspire myself about how change happens in society.

I recalled my early years of finding a hero in John Kennedy, and I searched to see if I could unearth a similar hero in science—someone who had engineered the kind of paradigm shift that Kuhn had described. Einstein had called Galileo the father of modern physics—indeed of modern science. I explored Galileo's life to discover how he confronted the dominant thinking of his times and found my mentor.

As I scoured accounts of Galileo's life, I hoped I would find strength of character, and I did. I thought I would find a fresh angle on the physical world, and I did. Wasn't Galileo quoted as describing wine as "light, captured by moisture?"

He prodded people to view nature not as received wisdom, but as facts based on observed behavior. He used his power of reason to demonstrate that repeated scientific observation can be the basis for knowledge. And though Galileo held firm to a faith in God, he also demonstrated that facts must slough the trappings of blind belief. The Church authorities in his time, as do many religious authorities in these times, too, did not yield easily to the potential of individuals finding truth for themselves. Famously, Galileo brooked the Inquisition by recanting his scientific observations and then whispered as he left the room where he had faced his accusers, "Still, it moves," referring to the earth revolving around the sun.

I thought I had my hero. I could relate to Galileo because I remembered being that adolescent who thought differently from what the preacher said. The chasm between my youth and the wisdom of elders echoed some of what Galileo might have faced when the Church confronted him.

But as I dug deeper into Galileo's life, I surprised myself to discover more than I looked for. I found Galileo's strong character spilled into arrogance. He made sport of his tormentor Pope Urban III. He made his detractors into simpletons and publicly ridiculed them in dialogues and debates. His actions made me wonder what would have happened inside the Church if Galileo had been capable of advancing his scientific principles while also demonstrating respect for his adversaries.

In my organization, I had been arguing that individuals and society could use the scientific method to discover the causes that lead people to violent sexual behavior. Then we could test and evaluate ideas that address those causes. But I sensed the public's consciousness seemed to volley from denial to terror. Sexual abuse either didn't exist, or without their vigilance, it would happen anytime and anywhere. The facts had formed a tinderbox of dry fuel that burst into flame when fanned with new information. I asked myself, as I had wondered about Galileo, what would happen inside our families and our society if we treated all those involved in a violent situation, even those who appeared to be our adversaries, with understanding and respect?

Could Kuhn's ideas answer this question? The scientific method had a structure for dealing with the problem. Facts add up to create new theory, but they alone do not result in change. Science does not answer to people's deepest fears or hopes.

I drew back and thought again of my childhood faith. I recalled its limitations, with the church's narrow vision of God as the only light at tunnel's end. I felt again the squelching pressure to attend youth group on Friday, church on Sunday morning, and Bible study that night. I thought about the way church excluded people who were not "believers," by using such passages from the Bible as "...don't cast your pearls before swine."

But I also remembered the messages of love, the way we were encouraged to find meaning in a "peace that passeth understanding," the love of God for each person. I remembered the women long ago in Sunday School teaching me how to love others, and learning that love heals sorrow and embraces our most profound difficulties.

I remembered how love had felt in my family: muddy. Like endless generations stretching back in time, I was raised by people who did not know how to express it. Although it must have happened, I cannot recall a single time my mother said, "I love you," unless I said it first. I remember my mother catching my hand to cross Main Street on John Kennedy's election day perhaps because I cannot remember any other times when she spontaneously expressed herself with caresses of her children.

My mother reined in loving actions and words, but the commitment inside her was steady, secure, and trustworthy. Her kind of love was unseen, but deeply felt by me and my siblings. It prepared me to discover a world where something very, very important is unseen but deeply felt. Not known, but deeply sensed.

I have faced many trials in my long life that have felt larger than what I have known or can handle, sometimes many in a day. At times I have felt faint, afraid. But then a sweet grace appears and I ride the current flowing unseen inside me. The movement is unmistakable, always available. Palpable. Putting names to it seems extraneous: God, Yahweh, Allah, Atman, the void that informs the Buddha. This is the world of faith, which is love.

Science cannot tread the path of this world. Perhaps Albert Einstein said it best when he was asked about the implications his theory of relativity had on religion. His answer: none, because relativity is a purely scientific matter.

The power of science lay in proofs upon proofs. The power of a spiritual life lies in what cannot be proven.

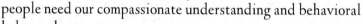

Preventing violence cannot base itself only on a study of behavior, no matter how rigorous. Nor can it depend solely on a faith that individuals who have harmed others can be loved back into society. We need to harness both the tools of science and the power of faith. Healthy people do not harm themselves or others. Unhealthy people need our compassionate understanding and behavioral help to change.

Thinking back five hundred years to Galileo's time, I understand that science and reason helped our world shed itself of ignorant belief. The world as we know it would not exist if those brave thinkers had lost their courage. Visiting again with Thomas Kuhn, I wonder about a way to reconcile faith and reason. Later in his life, in the essay *The Essential Tension*, Kuhn called upon scientists to act simultaneously as traditionalists and iconoclasts. Kuhn recognized that scientists could dare revolutionary advances if their science firmly rooted itself in current theory.

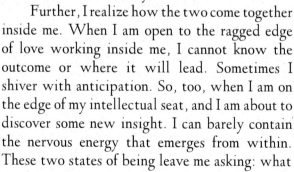

Further, I realize how the two come together inside me. When I am open to the ragged edge of love working inside me, I cannot know the outcome or where it will lead. Sometimes I shiver with anticipation. So, too, when I am on the edge of my intellectual seat, and I am about to discover some new insight. I can barely contain the nervous energy that emerges from within. These two states of being leave me asking: what will happen next? It is just the kind of challenge that human beings are perfectly evolved for.

John Kennedy led us with his own faith and reason when he raised aspirations of people all over the globe and put those aspirations to work. He created a Peace Corps to bring hope to struggling communities; he funded the science which sent mankind to the moon. John Kennedy saw deeply into who we were and by doing so helped us be more than we had been.

We, too, can stand firmly on ground that vibrates with tension between what we know and what we do not. The challenge for this century will include how reason *and* faith will advance civilization. When science, with its firm foundation in reason, goes arm in arm with connection, with its basis in faith, wisdom will manifest and humanity will leap forward.

PATRONS OF POSSIBILITY

A FEW years ago I flew to Florence, Italy to soothe my heart. At that time, I struggled with trying to accomplish a goal which seemed impossible. My resilience felt sapped; my usual sturdy constitution, tender. I sought what other seekers have found in that medieval city made famous by its cradling of the Renaissance: beauty in voluptuous abundance.

I made no plans in advance. I pored over no guidebooks, knew little about what treasures lay in this gallery or in that church. I guessed that I would uncover the bounty I needed if I simply were open without looking, if I wandered and allowed myself to be caught. In a corner of my awareness nestled a few people I had studied: Galileo, Dante, and Michelangelo. Perhaps if I touched upon places where they had been, I could kindle something fresh in me.

On my first morning I asked at hotel reception where I should go if I were interested in science. The clerk directed me to the Museo di Storia della Scienza. A short walk later, I tapped my toes in front of the entrance, ready to be the first visitor of the day. Once inside I fingered the glass case holding a telescope that Galileo had made. I felt inspired by how he devised a way to track the movements of the planets and the stars and then used his observations to support a radical theory. I knew already about the searing skepticism he had faced and that he had not lived to see society embrace his views.

So spending a morning with his instruments in that museum near the Arno gave me time for the reverie I needed, not to fathom his achievement, but to allow myself some awe in the face of it. How does a person, surrounded by the constricting realities of society, chart a path her or his own? How does a society shift its awareness and give birth to possibility? I wanted to know.

My hours with Galileo whetted my appetite to forage elsewhere in Florence. I came upon the frescoes in the churches and museums, appreciating the saturated color in the paintings or the calming simplicity of religious scenes. Then, after days of silent absorption, I found myself held in place by a painting of Mary holding the infant Jesus. In a flash, I unearthed a shiny something in the renderings of the baby and his mother which I had been looking at all week.

In room after room at the Uffizi museum, I saw the child depicted in his mother's arms. Quite often the artist painted him as we might see a miniature man, firm muscled and featured. His face shone, reflecting the golden halo about his head. And in many paintings, men taking the form of the parent Joseph, the visiting Magi, the saints, or the prophets, bowed in reverence to this babe.

Suddenly I saw before me, not the historical infant Jesus, nor the Christ child in his religious setting, nor even a narrow depiction of Christianity itself, but a newborn that moved adults to prostrate themselves. Had males bowed to a baby before, especially one born into the meager circumstances of a stable? Had I seen grown men do it since? What were these men paying homage to? Could they have been bowing to what Galileo left behind as he advanced his theory?

Galileo, based upon his observations, shifted human beings from the center of the cosmos to its periphery because like Copernicus, he theorized that the sun, not the planet Earth, occupied the center of a solar system. Were Renaissance artists placing human beings back into a fledgling form to allow for a new resurgence of growth? What if, standing in front of the paintings, I were seeing the sacred rebirth of Western consciousness in its infancy, emerging out of the dark ages—the individual born into earthly awareness of itself? If so, perhaps the rise of consciousness could only have been brought forth in Western civilization at a place and at a time when the early gleanings of science were putting humans in their physical place, so to speak.

Later, when I walked the long corridor in the Galleria dell'Accademia to come upon Michelangelo's David towering over me, I saw the physical virility of that emergent awareness prepared to square off against the giant, Goliath. Was David throwing a stone at the past—those dark ages exhausted of hope? Dazzled, I let myself unite in spirit with Michelangelo and with the artists of five hundred years ago. They fostered a magnificent turning which cleared the path for modern existence. Perhaps it occurred beyond ordinary human awareness, a kind of evolutionary force which had to push consciousness out if its womb.

In such an awakening, the role of a Galileo or of any individual artist, even Dante or Michelangelo, could not be planned or managed. And the whole endeavor—despite the beautiful results—could be a harrowing mess with its attendant screams. The lives of the people I had studied were fraught with distraction or hounding by the authorities. Many others around them were opposed, especially those in the dominant institution of the time, the church. In a frenzied attempt to curb change, the monk Savonarola took over the city of Florence for four years and ordered books and paintings burned in the city square until he himself died at the stake. And yet, I realized while I walked those same Florentine streets, that the evidence of the rebirth, nonetheless, had cascaded down through the ages.

So as I pondered these things, my heart eased and softened. I thought of that iconic symbol of the baby born into a world of strife two thousand years ago. His message of humility had brought hope to a tired people. Fifteen hundred years later artists painted fresh images of that baby so that individual ideals could again emerge. Now I had refreshed my flagging spirit by opening myself to the message the creators in the Renaissance had brought me.

In feeling gratitude for their creation, I returned to my question at the science museum: what fosters new possibilities so that they can withstand the resistance of a society looking backwards? The abundant art and science did not spring full grown from the head of a Zeus figure. None of those creators owned means. Behind every building, painting, sculpture, or scientific discovery stood a Medici or a Pazzi, a member of the Wool Merchants Guild, or even a cardinal. I realized, almost as an epiphany, the power of philanthropy to cultivate and to bring to society the fresh vision, the uncreated. The learned and wealthy citizens of Florence embodied their role as partners in creation.

As my time in Italy came to a close, I wondered what our lives in western countries would be like if we had not had a Renaissance. I am not a scholar, so I cannot prove that we would not have had the language of Shakespeare, the thinking of the Enlightenment, the scientific revolution, or on its heels, the Industrial Revolution and the music of Germany. But I do know that without these developments, my life would feel as if it were mired in medieval times.

I left Florence in reverence to genius and skill, but I also carried home a well-deep appreciation for the people who gave of their largess and time and imagination to bring that latent brilliance to fruition. I came home to my work to prevent violence determined to renew my gratitude for patrons of possibilities.

I draw inspiration from the Renaissance because we need today a similar radical shift in consciousness. We need to give birth to a way of thinking that sees violent acts as preventable. We need again patrons like those in the Renaissance whose foresight and wealth can uphold ideas, offer succor when we lose hope, and provide the means to succeed.

I have paused at times to consider whether my own ideas about preventing violence contain vision or delusion. I feel visionary when I support the theory that most people will break their habits leading to violence when the conditions around them change for them to do so. My support arises from studying others' work and from contemplating my own experience and ideas. But such a thought-filled process, taken too far, can lead to the delusion inherent in rigid beliefs.

My ideas will develop into useful visions if I expose them to others who might agree or who might not, but who engage me to think coherently. These people encourage me to pursue my wholesome thoughts, to wonder aloud what a relationship would be like, what a community would be like, what my society would be like without destructive violence toward oneself or others. The person who asks what I am thinking, who hears me out, who engages me in an exchange of ideas: this person is a patron of possibility. Men or women like this in one's life are like compost in the soil. With such rich humus, the seedling flourishes to its utmost.

At other times we need patrons who see us in a spiritual light. They minister to our sore spots, the heart-ache. Perhaps we have witnessed too much violence, or experienced it ourselves and suffer the consequences. At these times, we might become ourselves again if someone could tend to us, perhaps with some empathy and a question. *I am sorry that you are suffering. Is there anything I could do to help you, to support you? Have you lost your faith in the goodness of yourself or others?*

Then too, as in Italy years ago, financial patronage fuels the engine of social change. Money feeds the research to develop new ideas and to test them. Once new solutions are shown successful, people will come round to a different belief. I think, for example, of Air Force officials who were concerned by the high rate of suicide in their service. They budgeted the funds and undertook a study of its causes and what might be done to change it. After a series of interventions which encouraged help-seeking behavior by Air Force individuals and families, one third fewer suicides occurred. The work accomplished in the Air Force has provided a model others have followed.

I have come to honor the exchange between the giver and the given-to because I have seen the power of philanthropy bring my own ideas to light. I would not have created organizations without the steady belief of a tiny handful of mostly private people who each year wrote checks. Their generosity flowed from the wealth in their bank accounts. No one compelled them to give, and yet they did.

I have come to appreciate businesses of all kinds which succeed in our market system. In its most beneficial form, companies not only deliver a good or service to society and provide livelihoods for people, but also return shareholder value that supports civil society and social change. I have learned from the people who give what is the best way to do it. They say, "I trust in your work. I want to see you take your ideas forward." Their faith in me gives me the courage to keep going.

Even institutional foundations have blessed me with a few such personal touches. Early in my years hurting and hunting for funds for the prevention organization I ran, I called a foundation director. He took my call and listened deeply. Then he drove three hours to visit me in my small office and listened some more. When he got up to leave he said that I could submit a proposal to his foundation. As I saw him to the door, I tried to hide the tears of relief that came to my eyes. Even at that early point in my organization's life, I had weathered so many rejections by foundation staff.

I asked him what he had heard that interested him the most. With his hand on the knob, he peered at me, "You offer sound ideas, Fran, and ones that must be tried even if they do not work. My foundation invests in people. People who have a history of accomplishing what they set out to do and the courage to put their ideals into action. So don't be afraid of your leadership because thinking without action will not make change." He bolstered me. I wish experiences like this for every capable person.

The kinds of patronage I describe here, support for ideas, elevating the spirit of the idealist, and financial giving all benefit from a personal touch. Such touches mean even more for those working in the field of violence prevention. We cannot know who we help. When we work to keep an act of violence from ever occurring, we do not know the person who benefits from our days of labor—the person who might have been harmed but is not. The person who is whole, instead of broken, at the end of the day also does not know us, and what we have done in her behalf. We in this field need to build resilience to choose such a life, for it will not come with expressions of appreciation from those we have helped.

When I think of preventing violence, I see our society now as living in a kind of dark ages. I have held conversations with so many people who believe violence is part of the human condition, immutable. I wonder if collectively we feel hopeless, like I felt in the months before I traveled to Italy. We need images of renewal to inspire ourselves toward new possibilities.

I think again about the Magi who came to bow before the newborn. If they had not brought the gifts of their attention and wealth, would that infant have become a symbol of renewal? Signaling the end of the dark ages, the Medici risked their fortunes to foster beauty and truth—to the highest ideals. Now it is up to us to resist squandering our wealth on endless comforts, pleasures, or on ways to stay young, but instead to use our wealth to fuel the next Renaissance.

Patronage can be money; it can be enthusiasm and presence of mind; it can be champions who loan their power to build credibility. Every single person matters. I am a patron of possibility when I turn toward the light, toward hope and what helps, toward prevention. Will you turn, too?

OTHER TITLES BY EAST BRANCH PRESS

Flame Jewel Friend: A Triptych on Loss & Love
by Frances Henry, 2006

Uncommon Gifts by Ann L. Hallstein, 2007

The author appreciates editing by Lisa Oram of Amherst, Massachusetts, as well as printing and design by Ed Rayher of Swamp Press.

FRANCES HENRY was raised in Sag Harbor, New York. She works to prevent violence and writes essays from her home on the East Branch of the Westfield River in Cummington, Massachusetts.

WALTER KORZEC is a painter and printmaker living in Cummington, Massachusetts.

COLOPHON

This first edition was digitally prepared at Swamp Press during the March that would not let go. The type is Goudy's Deepdene. Many thanks to Walter Korzec for the use of his drawings and his tolerance of my graphic interpretive mode. The text was printed digitally at Collective Copies of Amherst on Royal Fiber. The flyleaf is UV Ultra, the cover stocks Classic Laid. The die cutting & letterpress cover printing was done at Swamp Press in Northfield, as was the Smyth sewing and subsequent gluing. This is one copy in a run of two hundred and fifty.